W9-CPE-599

Milk

WONDER
STARTERS

Milk

Pictures by CHRISTINE SHARR

Published by WONDER BOOKS
A Division of Grosset & Dunlap, Inc.
A NATIONAL GENERAL COMPANY
51 Madison Avenue   New York, N.Y. 10010

About Wonder Starters

Wonder Starters are vocabulary controlled information books for young children. More than ninety per cent of the words in the text will be in the reading vocabulary of the vast majority of young readers. Word and sentence length have also been carefully controlled.

Key new words associated with the topic of each book are repeated with picture explanations in the Starters dictionary at the end. The dictionary can also be used as an index for teaching children to look things up.

Teachers and experts have been consulted on the content and accuracy of the books.

Published in the United States by Wonder Books, a Division of Grosset & Dunlap, Inc., a National General Company.

ISBN: 0-448-09651-X (Trade Edition)
ISBN: 0-448-06371-9 (Library Edition)

FIRST PRINTING 1972

© Macdonald and Company (Publishers), Limited, 1971, London. All rights reserved.

Printed and bound in the United States.

I drink a glass of milk a day.
I drink all this milk in one year.

1

The milk I drink comes from cows.
Cows eat grass to help make milk.
2

Some people drink goats' milk.
Goats need less grass than cows.

3

This animal is called a llama.
In Peru people drink llamas' milk.
4

camel

yak

sheep

reindeer

Some people drink milk
from these animals, too.

5

Babies drink milk.
Mothers make milk for their babies.
6

Animals that make milk for their babies
are called mammals.
A cow is a mammal.

cat

monkey

horse

elephant

pig

Here are some more mammals.
They all make milk for their babies.
8

A few mammals swim in the sea.
These animals are all mammals.

9

Most people drink cows' milk.
This farmer is milking his cow.

10

The cow makes milk in its udder.
The milk comes from the teats.

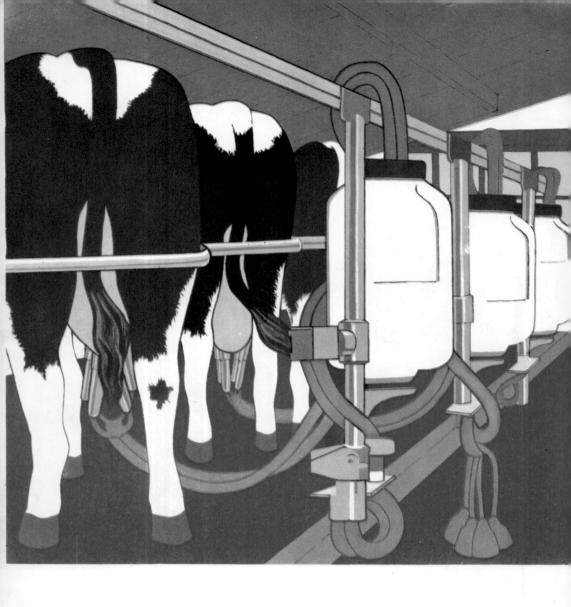

Most cows are milked by machine.

The milk goes into a milk truck.
The milk truck goes to the dairy.

13

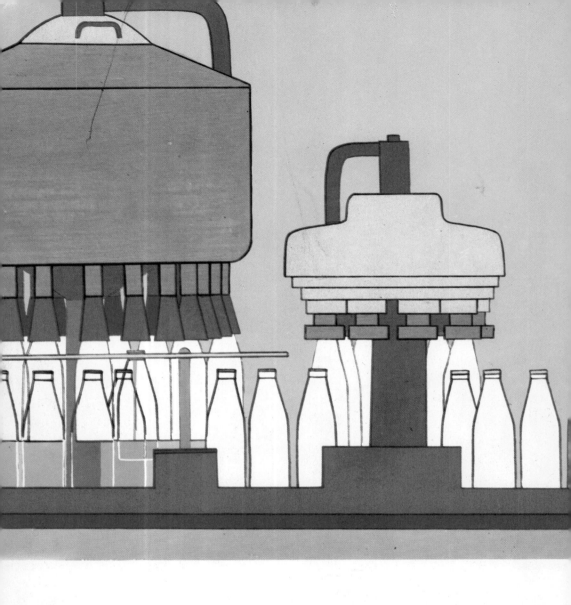

A machine puts the milk into bottles
at the dairy.
14

Milk is good for you.
Athletes drink lots of milk.

Mommy uses milk for cooking.
She makes all these things with milk.
16

Milk can go sour.
Cold milk stays fresh longer.

Cheese is made from milk.
There are many kinds of cheeses.
18

Cream comes from milk.
Butter is made from milk.

Sometimes milk is dried.
Water makes it into milk again.
Soldiers sometimes use dried milk.
It keeps well.

There was once a queen
who put milk in her bath.

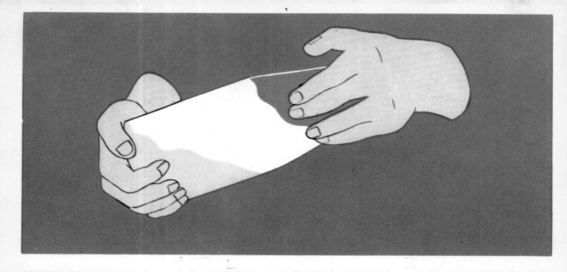

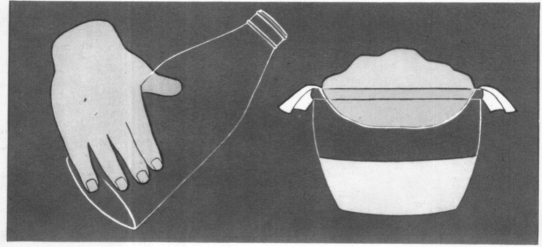

<u>See for yourself.</u>
Ask Mommy to shake up
some cream in a bottle.
When butter is formed, pour
it out through a cloth.

22

Starter's **Milk** words

goat
(page 3)

reindeer
(page 5)

llama
(page 4)

pig
(page 8)

camel
(page 5)

monkey
(page 8)

yak
(page 5)

walrus
(page 9)

sheep
(page 5)

whale
(page 9)

seal
(page 9)

farmer
(page 10)

udder
(page 11)

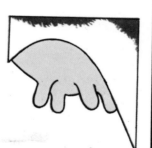

teat
(page 11)

milk truck
(page 13)

dairy
(page 13)

cheese
(page 18)

cream
(page 19)

butter
(page 19)

dried milk
(page 20)